Accreditation:
A Hands-On Approach for Principals

Second Addition

BY

THOMAS L. WHITTLE, Ed. D.

Principal and Retired Sergeant Major

Accreditation a Hands On Approach for Principals

iUniverse books may be ordered through booksellers or by contacting:

iUniverse
1663 Liberty Drive
Bloomington, IN 47403
www.iuniverse.com
844-349-9409

Because of the dynamic nature of the Internet, any web addresses or links contained in this book may have changed since publication and may no longer be valid. The views expressed in this work are solely those of the author and do not necessarily reflect the views of the publisher, and the publisher hereby disclaims any responsibility for them.

Any people depicted in stock imagery provided by Getty Images are models, and such images are being used for illustrative purposes only. Certain stock imagery © Getty Images.

ISBN: 978-1-6632-3075-1 (sc)
978-1-6632-3076-8 (e)

Library of Congress Control Number: 2021922310

Print information available on the last page.

iUniverse rev. date: 10/29/2021

Accreditation:
A Hands-On Approach for Principals

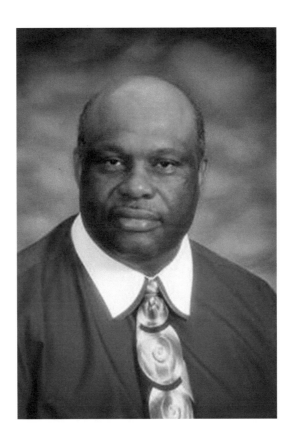

Dr. Thomas Whittle, Sergeant Major Retired
Biography

Dr. Thomas Whittle was born in Mecklenburg County, Virginia in January 1948. He graduated from East End High School in South Hill, VA in 1966, and from the University of Maryland University College at College Park with a Bachelor of Science in Business and Management in June 1992. He received his Master of Education degree from Virginia State University at Petersburg, VA in December 1996; he received his Master's in Divinity from Virginia Union University Samuel DeWitt Proctor School of Theology, May 2002, and he received his Doctor of Education degree in May 2011, also from Virginia State University. Dr. Whittle's dissertation topic: The Impact of Student Participation in Extra Curricular Activities on Academic Achievement.

After high school, Dr. Whittle joined the United States Army, he rose through the enlisted ranks to reach the top rank of Sergeant Major (SGM) and retired after 26 years of active service. He served three tours of duty in the Republic of Vietnam where he earned the Silver Star for heroism, two Purple Heart Medals, four Bronze Stars for Meritorious service, and the Combat Infantryman's Badge (CIB). He served sixteen years in Germany as a tank commander, platoon sergeant, first sergeant, battalion master gunner, division master gunner, USAEUR master gunner, and G3 sergeants major for 8th ID, and CSM of 1/9 Air Calvary Squadron Fort Lewis Washington. Upon retiring, Dr. Whittle entered the field of education as a teacher of mathematics in Nottoway, VA; he later became principal of Nottoway Middle School, Nottoway High School, John F. Kennedy High School in Richmond VA, Petersburg High School in Petersburg, VA, HD Woodson (STEM) High School in Washington DC, and Antilles High School in Puerto Rico. He is also the author of Accreditation a Hands-on Approach for Principals (2007), presented at the national High Schools That Work (HSTW) conference in Nashville Tennessee on the topic: The use of classroom student performance data to improve teacher instructional practices. Dr. Thomas Whittle is also DoDEA's Secondary Principal of the year for 2018.

DEDICATION

This book is dedicated to my family. My parents, Conrad L., and Nancy Louise Whittle, who supported me in my youth, instilled in me the value of education, and made me the person I am today. My late brother, Reverend Conrad Odell Whittle, who motivated, encouraged, and taught me the value of demanding work. Kristina, my Wife who is a skilled educator and accompanied me through the writing process. A special debt of gratitude is extended to my oldest daughter, Tomalyn, who was a student and graduated seventh in her class at Nottoway High School where I served as principal.

Finally, to the faculty of Antilles High School in Puerto Rico, Dr. Reginald Edwards, Ms. Erin Crossan, Ms. Leilan Hamm, and Ms. Joi Gause Assistant Principal Fort Campbell High School for their support. I would like to thank the faculties and staffs of Nottoway High and Nottoway Middle schools of Nottoway, Virginia, John F. Kennedy High School of Richmond, Virginia; King George Middle School of King George, Virginia; and Petersburg High School of Petersburg, Virginia, and Antilles High School Puerto Rico, for their patience, kindness, and encouragement. My thanks go to my cohort members and Dr. Richardson, Dr. Jones, Dr. Griffin, Dr. Osa, and Dr. Norman, who encouraged me to author this book. I appreciate all the guidance and recommendations from those who worked closely with me in my literary effort.

Acknowledgements

I would like to thank the faculties and staffs of Nottoway High and Nottoway Middle schools of Nottoway, Virginia; John F. Kennedy High School of Richmond, Virginia; King George Middle School of King George, Virginia; and Petersburg High School of Petersburg, Virginia, and Antilles High School Puerto Rico for their patience, kindness, and encouragement. My thanks go to my cohort members and professors Dr. Richardson, Dr. Jones, Dr. Griffin, Dr. Osa, and Dr. Norman, who served as my dissertation committee and encouraged me to author this book.

The School Principal and Accreditation
School Improvement: An Ongoing Process

CONTENTS

Preface

To the Educational Leaders at Building Level

Leadership is an art form that has been practiced since the beginning of time, however it is not an exact science in which any person with a certain amount of education and some type of a checklist can guarantee student academic success. The highly recommended solutions from great educational leaders of yesterday (such as Plato, Aristotle, Jefferson, Washington, and Socrates) do not work in all situations. These successful leaders did not just lead their followers; they taught them various leadership principles for given situations. Successful principals learn through experiences what works in a particular situation and what does not work. Remember, one can learn from a failure as well as through accomplishment. Each time you fail, it provides you with the opportunity to learn and be successful.

Building principals who have mastered the art of leadership do not rely on trial and error. This Hands-On Approach for Principals provides a small resource for continuous improvement in the art of building-level leadership. The small summary of my experiences may serve as a springboard for each principal's self-awareness and discovery.

This resource will assist you with the analysis of leadership situations in your building and in systematically choosing a leadership style which best fits the situation (Reflective, Relational, Collaborative, Communicative or Visionary). When you have developed an understanding of these various techniques, situations will dictate the application of each technique. You will make better decisions and that will lead to a motivated faculty and student body. This gives you a much greater chance of leading your building to student academic success.

Leadership is about change; embedded in your leadership is the hope of the students. You are standing on the shoulders of great educational leaders of yesterday, looking into the future, and seeing possibilities. Face change with a smile; embrace change with determination unseen by those around you. I believe it was Reverend Doctor Martin Luther King who said, "The best leaders are determined, bold, and reject inhibitors imposed by old traditions and habits." Moving your school to full accreditation will not be easy; your goals must be clearly stated. Remember, the simplest approach will prove to be the most effective. Respect all points of view and do not set your standards too low. Find one thing in your school where all stakeholders, even the extremists, can visualize the school climate and culture better because of its success. The goal of this book is to aid you in your attempt to accreditate your school. Do not allow misguided teachers the opportunity to rob students of their academic successes and joy at the completion of your mission.

Introduction

The School Board Meeting

The story begins in a small south-central county in Virginia. It was one evening at a school board meeting where the principals had to tell what they would do to improve the Standards of Learning test scores, which were awful in five schools in the county. The meeting moved along well with each principal telling what he or she would do to improve test scores. Finally, the high school principal came to the podium and was questioned by the board concerning Algebra I and II scores, which were 15% and 9% respectively. He was unprepared to answer the puzzling questions and respond to the harsh criticism. The next set of questions by the board was directed to poor performance of the students in Social Studies Standards of Learning. These scores were 25% and included World Geography, World History I, World History II, and Virginia and US History.

The principal became red faced and said, "Pick a number; what do you want the scores to be?" The board was flabbergasted, and the members of the board looked at each other with a sense of disbelief. Parents were astonished that the principal would make such a statement. The future of the children of the county was on the line. The newspaper persons were quick to print the demise of the principal. Little did the principal, the board, parents, teachers, and other attendees know, the high school principal was right. The school division had gone through years of staff development; however, there was no process for remediation of students who were unsuccessful academically. There was no process of assisting teachers with the implementation of the best pedagogical strategies in their classroom. The principal asked the right question because there was no implementation of a school improvement plan directed toward African American achievement. There was no plan to assist students who needed a little additional academic help, therefore, each year the principals, central administrators, and school board members were wishing for improved student achievement without a plan. They were like a carpenter going to build a split-level home without a blueprint (picture of the finished product).

There was no plan for academic success, there was no vision, no conceptual understanding of how to disaggregate student academic data. Teachers were left year after year repeating the same mistakes without a proven method of data collection and analysis. Sure, they had the data from the previous years SOL tests; however, they were teaching new students. The data they had received was for their previous students who had moved on to the next grade with holes in their learning without having an opportunity for remediation. There was no plan, there was no conceptual framework for remediation, there was no understanding of flexibility in scheduling to facilitate opportunities for remediation, and there was no willingness on the part of the teachers to take responsibility for student learning. They continued to blame the students for not having background knowledge of content.

Being an older man but young in the business of education and school leadership, I sat there and observed the sequence of events. I wondered if I had the skill set necessary to meet the challenges and demands of school accreditation. I knew about Virginia Department of Education's web page and all the information and resources available. I knew about data disaggregation; I had learned this skill from Dr. James Haywood, a physicist who worked at Virginia Department of Education.

The process of turning a school around academically began for me at that board meeting. There are several things a leader must have a good handle on before he or she can begin the turn around process:

- Where is the relevant student academic data (Criterion Reference data, not SAT, ACT, and or Stanford 9)? Those data might be helpful, but they do not tell the story of a school you are trying to turn around and move to accreditation. You are not looking for national ranking data but criterion reference data (data on taught content).
- Where is the discipline data, where did most disciplinary incidents occur, between which groups (boys or girls, white or black), and in what part of the building did each type of incident happen?

- Do the teachers know the content and where (what university) to get help to determine an answer to this question?
- Can the teachers disaggregate data and provide an analysis of what the data is saying for their tests given in their classrooms?
- Can teachers manage their classrooms (classroom management)?

This book describes the basic steps I took in five different schools to achieve excellent academic success: four out of the five schools made astronomical academic gains and four out of the five are accredited. This book chronicles the actions of department chairpersons, assistant principals, and teachers in general. There were no magic wands, no extreme teaching models used, and no great leaders hired by the school board. This process is the one that any principal or school-based administrator can implement to take his or her school through an improvement process.

The school board meeting was about meeting the requirements of the federal law "No Child Left Behind" (NCLB) Act and closing the achievement gap between white students and other minority student groups in the school district. All school districts must develop effective strategies to meet the NCLB goals of excellence, equity, and high expectations for all students in the respective school divisions. As I reflected on the school turn-around process, a few critical themes emerged: Teacher accountable for student learning, instructional process, alignment of curriculum with standards and assessment, pacing charts, and internal collaboration.

CHAPTER 1

PROBLEM SOLVING PROCESS: A STRATEGY FOR SUCCESS

The major problem with school accreditation is that most school divisions, central office-level leaders did not recognize that there was a problem with student achievement until "No Child Left Behind" legislation was passed and signed under President Bush. Few, if any, educators recognized this law as the reauthorization of the Elementary and Secondary Education Act (ESEA) of 1965. The law focused the light of academic achievement on each subgroup within a school district. The law required that each subgroup show increased academic achievement in comparison to the majority group (white). NCLB (2001) was enacted to update the 1965 (ESEA) as part of President Lyndon B. Johnson's War on Poverty. ESEA is the nation's major source of dollars for kindergarten through twelfth grade. ESEA appropriation totals about eleven billion dollars annually. This single act has been sending federal dollars to states in support of poor schools, communities, and children for four decades (ESEA, 1965). NCLB has four major principles that determine its funding: focus on what works (best practices), increase accountability for student academic performance, empowerment of parents, and reduce bureaucracy.

This new law called for spending money in education and making certain that any funding is associated with academic success. The law directed extensive revamping of state and local school systems and the federal government would invest billions of dollars nation-wide to aid in the implementation process. According to U. S. Department of Education (2001), the intent of the ESEA has remained unaffected since its ratification: To ensure education opportunity for all children regardless of socioeconomic background, and to close the achievement gap between poor and affluent children by providing additional resources for schools serving disadvantaged students.

The law required states and local school divisions to revamp their approach to educating children. The federal government pledged billions of dollars to aid states with the implementation of the law. In the law there are additional requirements of teachers to be "highly qualified," meaning they had to have a degree in the area they are teaching and past both parts of the PRAXIS examination. An additional goal of NCLB is to increase academic achievement in math, science, and technology, and to ensure all students can read by third grade. Each state must participate in the National Assessment of Educational Progress (NAEP) for reading and math with the intent of validating state test results. The most important part of NCLB is the "adequate yearly progress" (AYP). The term AYP means the number of students scoring at or above proficient level on the examination must increase yearly to meet the federal government's acceptable benchmark. Academically challenged schools that failed to meet AYP over time were in danger of sanctions that became increasingly severe with yearly failure of all subgroups to demonstrate academic improvement.

Low-performing schools that fail year after year to meet or exceed AYP benchmarks faced a wide array of punitive sanctions. Schools that failed to meet benchmarks in consecutive years received technical assistance from the district; these schools were required to develop an improvement plan and provide students with school of choice. Schools that did not meet benchmarks in three years were required to develop an improvement plan, provide school of choice, and provide supplemental education services to low achieving and disadvantaged students. The students' parents could choose the services from a list of state approved venders, which may include private tutors. The money to support this effort came from set-aside funds from the school district's budget. After the fourth year of not meeting AYP benchmarks, more strenuous sanctions take effect, which include corrective action such as relevant staff being replaced, appointing outside experts to advise the school, and implementation of a new curriculum or reconstitution of the school (U. S. Department of Education, 2001).

As data began to emerge from various states' high stakes tests and the accountability for this data, the reality of poor academic achievement on the part of many minority groups became evident, and educational leaders sought ways to explain why this group was not achieving. Educational leaders were not accustomed to being criticized concerning the academic achievement of African American students. Once the problem of minority achievement (Achievement Gap) was realized, there was no process available to analyze the cause of the gap.

The reauthorization of ESEA as NCLB forced local administrators to take a serious look at the complete population within the school district. Leaders in the field of education could no longer camouflage their statistical data to hide the minority groups. For the first time in the educational history of the United States, each subgroup within a school division would now have its data disaggregated and displayed against the majority groups; real academic success was being measured, and principals and teachers were being held accountable.

As educational leaders, principals were being asked to solve the problem of academic achievement for all students, minorities included. One of the major steps in solving any problem is to **recognize that there is a problem**. The disaggregated data indicated that there was a problem between black and white student achievements. The second step in the problem-solving process is **evaluation of the data for trends, whether positive or negative**. The trends may be systemic or a function of curriculum alignment, teacher preparation, school climate, school culture, learned curriculum versus taught curriculum, assessed curriculum versus written curriculum, or a lack of differentiated instruction. After the analysis of the data, the third step in the problem-solving process is to **develop a proposed solution and try the developed solution on a small portion of the student population.** The fourth step of the process is to **make corrections of the proposed solution as the data comes in from the small student experiment.** The fifth step in the process is to try the **successful solution over the entire school population and replicate the process in all content areas.** The final step in the problem-solving process is to **document and report academic achievement successes to the educational community.** Reeves (2006) discusses his interpretation of school-level leadership as creating a leadership map. The map would allow a school leader to replicate his or her success and change the failures to successes. I believe without some systematic way of documenting successes or failures, school-based leaders would be setting themselves up for continuous failure.

The achieved successes of the students who have gone through this process should be shared with the national educational community. In sharing **data** with other communities and schools, districts will assist in closing the academic achievement gap between blacks and whites.

CHAPTER 2

THE SECRET OF GOOD ORDER AND DISCIPLINE IN SCHOOLS

There were several problems dealing with teaching that I had to address in each school where I was principal. The most profound was student discipline. Teachers were unable to teach because of student disruptions. Teachers were competing with students to gain the attention of other students in the classroom. Strict discipline measures were implemented to support teachers, and staff development was instituted to assist teachers who needed assistance in classroom management. A school division that is serious about accreditation cannot allow a few disruptive students to prevent other students from learning and achieving. Teachers were unaware of what good discipline meant and students were comfortable with disrespecting teachers. The five different school divisions where I was principal had a challenging time recruiting, hiring, and retaining quality teachers because of weak administrators and non-support by local school board members. Many of the teachers who stayed on staff were weak teachers and wanted their students to sit in lines and rows without making any noise. Therefore, I created a handout with an explanation of what good order and discipline entailed.

This handout was the foundation for school-wide change in each school division during my principalship. Teachers who had taught for many years said that they were enjoying teaching again and their students where achieving. Setting the tone in discipline sent a clear message to all involved that we believed students could achieve and we expected each student to play a significant role in the school reaching full accreditation. Embedded in the handout are the learning styles of each student, whether a student was an auditory, visual, or tactile learner.

HAND-OUT FOR SCHOOL INSTRUCTIONAL SUCCESS

What is good order? Teachers would have less difficulty keeping order in their classrooms if there were a clearer picture of what good order means.

When I was a lad, I traveled to a wheat-grinding mill with my father. We arrived at the end of the day, and I was amazed at the total silence. It was eerie and almost unnatural. Gigantic grinding stones were motionless and silent. Massive blowers were mute. The mill seemed stationary and in a state of limbo. The inactivity substituted the sounds I had anticipated, and silence itself seemed unnatural and deafening. For a boy who had expected the sounds of production, it was spooky. I was also disappointed that the plant was not living up to its usual potential and was not turning out a product.

As I revisit the mill subconsciously, I discover that teachers should not expect student productivity from order that results in silent, dormant, and inactive students.

This is not the type of order teachers should want in a classroom. Students do not need to be in a state of limbo with their minds silent and no product produced. Teachers should not want to change pupils into silent rows of inert grinding stones and deactivated blowers, which receive and produce nothing.

Teachers can learn from the master of the wheat-mill. They must be vigilant in differentiating between the reassuring hum of learning and progress. They must be attentive for the sound of silence that may indicate that there is disorder and lifeless rows of potential waiting to hum. Teachers should want the sounds of life in their classrooms. The steady hum indicates that learning activities and diverse teaching strategies are meeting the needs of all students in the classroom.

Another secret to keeping order in the classroom is securing and holding the attention of students immediately upon their entrance into the room. When students are totally engaged by the lesson, they will not have time to think about mischief. Students may not be demonstrating an upright posture or have their feet placed properly on the floor, but if they are engaged in learning and the expectations are established instantly, the hum of learning commences.

Students can be compared to young ponies. When one holds the pony firmly by the bridle, the pony is usually perfectly obedient. The firm grasp tells the pony that his master is in charge. If the master relaxes his grasp on the pony's bridle, the pony will become restless. If the master lets go of the bridle, the pony is off in a flash. If a teacher engages the interest of students by taking them firmly by the bridle at the beginning of class, they will be focused on the business of learning. The teacher can relax the bridle now and then but must be able to regain control in an instant. When control of the bridle is totally dropped, disorder and confusion may occur. Teachers need to engage their students for the entire instructional period and be prepared to facilitate the learning process even before the students arrive in the classroom.

Teachers must plan activities that will last the entire time that students are in class. Lessons, demonstrations, and activities must be varied throughout the entire class period to keep students' minds fully engaged. To facilitate the learning process, teachers should have a detailed knowledge of all the learning styles of their students and plan activities that meet the needs of all the students who are in their assigned classes. Teachers need to maintain the momentum through the daily lesson plan and throughout the hands-on activity and curriculum.

Teachers who work in school divisions where the 4x4-block schedule is used are particularly challenged to keep students engaged and maintain order. A long class period can quickly deteriorate into disorder when there is no solid plan, no varying of activities, and no way of accommodating learning styles. Institutions responsible for teacher preparation must educate young men and women to teach effectively within the 4x4-block schedule. New strategies, planning tools, devices, and learning activities need to be developed to assist teachers in meeting this challenge. Teachers are well educated in content but need to have additional tools at their disposal to address lesson structure and learning style needs of the culturally diverse classrooms of the new millennium.

Teachers want students to be about the business of learning. When teachers use the principles of the wheat-mill and the lesson of the pony in combination with effective methods, strategies, meaningful and relative learning activities, and proper disciplinary procedures student success will be realized. Teachers cannot say students do not know or do not have background knowledge; the new teachers must use their teaching skills by differentiating instruction, which will capture students where they are and teach old content along with the new.

The following step-by-step 4x4 or odd and even block instructional tools provide a framework for time allocation and incorporate learning styles for experienced and inexperienced teachers:

- **<u>Training Statement</u>**: State the purpose for this block of instruction. State the objective and write it on the board for the entire class to read, the teach should have an exemplar for students (2-5minutes).

- **<u>Caution Statement</u>**: If you are conducting a lab experiment that involves the use of chemicals or a shop class that involves the use of power equipment, you must make a cautionary statement regarding safety. If this step is not needed a warm-up activity can be used at this point (3-5 minutes).

- **<u>Pretest</u>**: This test is administered at the beginning of the lesson to measure students' understanding of previously taught material. The same test will be given at the end of the instructional block (8-15 minutes).

- **<u>Orientation Statement</u>**: This consists of a focus statement to get the students started on the task objective-(s). This is an enabling statement. For example, "At the end of this block you will be able to…" (8-10 minutes).
- **<u>Demonstration</u>**: Demonstrate the process of completing an exercise related to the class objective. Demonstrations may include working mathematics problems, constructing complete sentences, how to do a science experiment, etc.… (15-20 minutes).

- **Task Steps**: Demonstrate the process you are working on step by step. At the end of the step-by-step process, allow the students to ask questions (15-25 minutes).

- **Guided Practice/Cooperative Learning**: Students are allowed to practice the lesson at their own pace, teachers walk around and ask higher order questions. Students can do this individually, cooperatively in small groups, or with peer assistance (10-15 minutes).

- **Performance Test**: Administer a post-test that is the same as the pre-test. Conduct this activity at least three times per week.

- **Closure**: End the block of instruction with additional statements and information that will bring the day's lesson to a smooth close and prepare the students for the next day of instruction.

- **Required Resources**: Make certain that all the necessary instructional materials are present in the classroom to assist you with the lesson. Make certain that the technology operates well, and student have their tech equipment and it functions and that pens, pencils, paper, etc., are available for utilization by the students who do not have such items. Always have extra paper, pencils, pens, and so on, so that students will not have an excuse for not participating in classroom assignments.

Keep in mind this is one tool I used to achieve academic success in the schools where I was principal. The purpose of this tool was to create an instructional climate where all students could learn based on his or her learning style (visual, auditory, or tactile). It is important to ensure that every year in secondary school be used to prepare students for postsecondary education whether in a four-or two-year college, trade school, or **on-the-job-training (OJT)**. Looking at education, counselors on the secondary level should encourage students not to waste any time while preparing themselves for the world of work or continuing education. Students and parents should be made aware of the benefits of taking the rigorous courses such as Calculus, Trigonometry, Advanced Biology, dual enrollment course work, and other AP courses.

With a solid background in Mathematics and English, minority students will be prepared to take those challenging college courses that lead to successful careers. The intellectually competitive nature of our world makes it extremely important that as educators we waste no time in the educational process. Student self-discipline plays a key role, as well as good counseling. Placing students in a collaborative learning environment places the responsibility for learning on each student. The learning stage is students centered, students are asking each other higher order thinking questions and each student must explain her or his rational. Teachers should never ask a student a yes or no question, the questions should require an answer to why you think that way or where did you get that answer?

CHAPTER 3

BENCHMARK TESTS AND WHY THEY DON'T WORK

There is a new and old trend sweeping across the nation. School divisions are trying to beat the state tests that are used by the Federal Government and state mandated testing to determine Average Yearly Progress (AYP). Many superintendents have allowed curriculum specialists to persuade them to hire a person strictly for the purpose of testing coordinator. This person has the responsibility of scheduling, monitoring test results, and scheduling benchmark tests. The benchmark test is normally given to students each six or nine weeks depending on the report card schedule of a school division. Students and may teachers, and parents view the benchmark test as another test without any feedback; therefore, most students do not take the test seriously.

Testing serves two major purposes. One is to tell the student how he or she understands the materials that have been taught, and the other is to inform the teacher how well he or she is teaching the content and if the teaching strategies being used are effective. Wilson (2005) states that the *norm-referenced test* compares student performance against that of the norm-group. We want to compare students against the state or federal standards. The *criterion-referenced test* compares student performance to a standard; the purpose is not to rank order, but to classify students. A standard is set, for example for satisfactory or excellent, pass or fail performance, and each student's score is compared to that standard (the cut score). Most school divisions do well on the first purpose for testing. Student grades reflect passing or failing but teachers continue to teach the same way if large numbers of their students fail. Using benchmark testing for grading, central office feedback, and measuring student academic understanding is not the answer. When benchmark testing is used for grading at the end of the six- or nine-weeks grading period the test becomes another summative test. Students are required to take time and prepare for the test and, a small formative test would serve the purpose of determining the academic retention of each student. The formative assessment should be used as an ongoing assessment (weekly or bi-weekly) to check student understanding, at the completion of a thematic unit of instruction or at the completion of an objective. The formative assessment should be prepared prior to teaching the material, and it should be developed by teachers or by departments collectively. Teachers who are teaching the same course content should be required to use the same collaborative teacher-made assessment or rubric.

When I was in the military and had responsibility for soldiers' lives. I found out that most students could not do well on written tests but were able to demonstrate their mastery of the subject matter against a standard. The army published a Soldiers Manual of Common Tasks (SMCT), this manual had all the common task a soldier should be able to do at a given rank. The manual soldiers carried with them, and it kept a record of their mastery and the date of the assessment. The data wall provides this type of assessment.

Collaboration Among Teachers

Teachers working together at the same planning period is not collaboration. Teachers planning the master schedule and other coordinated school activities is not collaboration. While it is nice for people to get along in a work environment especially schools, the real measure of collaboration is student success. Collaboration, then is a commitment to student academic success and excellence against state standards at all costs. The process of collaborating brings about a deep discussion among teachers and administrators on what are the next steps and a plan of action for students who are not successful. The teachers who teach the unsuccessful students should be at the forefront of the process following a school-based plan. Teachers who teach the same content conduct a task analysis to fully understand where the learning gaps are and select a best practice strategy to assist the unsuccessful students. The process is so critical for teachers and students; the process should be scheduled in the master schedule, and nothing should supplant this meeting requirement.

The collaboration effort of teachers should always center around the four following basic questions:

1. What is it that we want our students to learn? The answer to this question starts with the standards.
2. How do we know if they have learned it? The answer to this question is assessment results.
3. What do we do if they did not learn it? The answer is remediating the students on what they did not learn by scaffolding their learning.
4. What do we do for those students who get it? Teach should provide enrichment activities around the same content.

Using the student formative assessment data will always provide a good indicator of where students are in their understanding. The other data which can provide a good starting point for teaches is PSAT data. The data give a longitudinal look at student subsets of performance in the areas of command of evidence, words in context, analysis in history/social studies, and science. The good part about this data is that the eight grade and ninth grade test are the same; the tenth and eleventh grade test are the same. The use of a data room where teachers can see a visualization of student data that helps in answering these questions. When teachers are assessing students with a formative assessment, the assessment should be one of agreed upon target scores for content mastery, example (85%) in algebra I classes. An organized data room is so important, it allows teachers to come together and see the students' scores who are not successful.

Using the data room also allows teachers to brainstorm root cause analysis (RCA) using visual data. The data room also serves as a location for teachers to meet weekly or as often as they deem necessary.

Differentiate Corrective Instruction

The most challenging aspect of using formative assessments is knowing what to do with the results. Results that indicate a student has not learned an important concept or skill call for corrective instruction and additional opportunities for the student to demonstrate learning.

"To be effective to the maximum extent possible, corrective teaching must be qualitatively different from the initial teaching," says Thomas Guskey (2005). "Little variation in the teaching results in great variation in student learning." If direct instruction was used for the initial lesson, a corrective lesson that makes use of manipulatives or a tactile or kinesthetic activity might be appropriate. Students can be grouped so that those who demonstrate understanding are provided with enrichment activities while those who need additional time are provided with follow-up instruction. Alternatively, pairing high-and-low-achieving students for a cooperative activity can benefit both learners as well. The aim is to reach all students by using a variety of teaching strategies.

The results from the formative assessments are used for remediation of those students who failed to meet the school set course content mastery percentage. In the schools where I was principal, students must have achieved 85% mastery of each objective. Their teachers scheduled students who did not meet this objective for remediation and results from the remediation sessions were recorded and turned in to the principal. The tool I used for recording the names of students that attended the remediation session is at appendix (A). In the words of Reeves (2006), "We provide a summative assessment at the end of the school year, which is too late to help those students who need the help, and the results come back when the students have moved on to another grade or teacher."

In Virginia, a state that uses writing and reading tests for verified credits (at the secondary level), these tests are normally given in the eleventh grade. Many school divisions have a special class for students who have trouble taking the reading and writing tests. English teachers can tell us at the beginning of each semester who can read and who can write. Many of those students remain in the classes and fail, but they take the writing and reading tests. To solve the problem, principals and department chairperson should institute reading and writing across the curriculum. I attended a workshop conducted by Mr. Larry Bell, and he addressed the way we teach African American boys and girls; teachers allow these students to skate by because many teachers do not want a confrontation with the parents of these students in reference to the student's lack of success. Mr. Bell said, "There are twelve words African American students have a problem with." The words confuse the students or throw them off from the real meaning of the question. When teachers use the words, they should call the words out and give concrete examples when using the words in instructions. The following is the list of words and the normal meaning:

- **Trace:** outline list, list steps
- **Analyze**: take it apart, think about it, study the pieces
- **Infer**: guess based on clues, what do you think about it, read between the lines
- **Evaluate**: judge, in your own words
- **Formulate**: create, put it together
- **Describe**: talk about it, paint me a picture, tell me all about it
- **Support:** prove reason, give me examples
- **Explain**: discuss, tell me about it, retell it to me in a short manner
- **Summarize**: retell main point, what its all about in your own words
- **Compare**: explain the differences
- **Contrast**: find differences (all the way that things are different or alike)
- **Predict**: what do you think will happen next.

The words require students to use higher ordered thinking skills as diagrammed in Bloom's Taxonomy. The students now must apply knowledge, provide a synthesis, analyze, and evaluate information. Any assessment given must meet the depth of knowledge (DOK) required by the standard.

I required the teachers to copy these words in **bold** print and post them in their classrooms. Each day teachers were expected to use these words in their content presentation. Teachers were expected to use the words in their assessments. I wanted teachers to make sure that parents were fully aware of how important these words were and how the words play a decisive role in their child's educational success. In the age of accountability, assessments are most important for teachers, administrators, and students. The assessment is critical for students because in most states a student's graduation from high school may depend on their success or failure of one given assessment. The assessment is important for teachers and administrators because of accountability to the federal government's (NCLB) and or the state developed end-of-course assessments or state benchmark cut scores in pass percentage.

Few of the teachers in elementary-or secondary-level schools understand benchmark assessments; therefore, they are not able to make adjustment in their instruction practices. Most school divisions have data persons to provide analysis and display their data analysis in some understandable manner, but the teachers are not required to analyze student data thus no change in instruction practices occur. Wilson (2005) states that teachers must understand what type of tests students are taking so they can better prepare students for the test. I offer this example: when my daughter, who is now twenty-four years old, took the drivers' license tests eight years ago, she studied the test book. She would not have been successful if she had not studied the test. The test was a *criterion reference test*; she was measured against a set state standard. I knew that she would receive questions relating to right of way, stopping distance, signs, and parking rules; therefore, it was necessary for her to study those types of questions from the book, which was the test.

I knew what would be on the test before my daughter took it. In Virginia, there is a blueprint of what is going to be on the Virginia Standards of Learning tests (SOLs). Teachers and administrators know what is going to be on the end of course test; therefore, there is no excuse for student failure. Wilson (2005) suggests that assessments are designed before the lesson. The teacher must determine what the student must be able to do at the conclusion of the lesson prior to determining the best instructional strategies to use to accomplish that goal. Standards for determining the quality of student work must also be established prior to instruction.

Wilson goes on to discuss assessments as more than a summative written evaluation. They are a continuous activity of observation by the teacher of activities by the student that provide feedback to students and teachers for the purpose of improving instruction and completing the picture of what a student knows. Knowledge is not simply abstract; brain research indicates that new things we learn must be attached to what we already know, so we can remember it for application at some later point in our lives. Students should know to what level of proficiency they are expected (**Setting High Expectations**) to know what you are teaching them. Rubrics should be designed prior to teaching students a task that requires stringent levels of competency.

The use of a rubric for grading removes the appearance of teacher favoritism, and students will work to the higher-level of expectation. Students are willing to work for an A if the standards and expectations are known prior to making the assignment. An example of a rubric is shown below. In this illustration of a narrative essay written using the Virginia Standards of Learning's Enhanced Scope and Sequence as a grading standard, students would know what the expected level of performance is to obtain any number grade through four. The grading scale is 1 through 4, 1 being the lowest and 4 being the highest. Students would have no problem understanding what the expected level of performance is to achieve any given number grade. When students have the rubric in advance, they can establish timelines for drafts of their narrative essays and get feedback from their teachers prior to the completion dates. The teacher will have an opportunity to go over student written work and give feedback to students to guide the writing process. The idea is that each student would write at the level to get an A, and the writing proficiency across the school would improve in all course content.

Essay Rubric

Narrative Essay Rubric Made from Virginia's Enhanced Scope and Sequence for English

	4	3	2	1
Organization	The narrative has a clear beginning, middle, and end. It starts with the most important event. It ends with the writer expressing his or her thoughts about the personal experience.	The narrative has a clear beginning, middle, and end. It begins with the most important event. It ends with the writer leaving out personal comments or experiences.	The narrative may be void of a clear beginning, middle, and end. It may have personal comments or thoughts; however, requires additional information or elaboration.	The writer may have left out a beginning, middle, and end. The essay may be void of any personal comments, thoughts, and/or reflection.
Elements of a Narrative	The narrative is clear and interesting with a main point. It is told in a chronological order; transition from point to point makes it clear; contains specific details about people, places, and events. The writer consistently uses first person point of view.	The narrative has a clear point. It is told in chronological order; transitions make the order clear. The narrative contains some specific details about people, places, and events; some may not be identified clearly enough for the intended reader. The writer sometimes uses first person point of view.	The narrative is told in a chronological order. Transitions are usually not used and it repetitive. There may not be enough details for the reader.	The narrative may not have any chronological order; there may not be sufficient details for the intended reader to get the point of the essay.
Grammar, Usage, Mechanics, and Spelling	There are very few errors in spelling, grammar, punctuation, and mechanics. The writer consistently uses first person pronouns, including me and my, correctly consistently.	There are some errors in grammar, spelling, mechanics, and punctuation. The writer usually uses first person pronouns.	There are more than the acceptable number of errors in grammar, spelling, mechanics, and punctuation. The writer mixes use of pronouns. Word choices in details are confusing for the reader.	Large number of errors in mechanics, spelling, grammar, and punctuation. Order and chronology may lack punctuation, which hinders reader comprehension.

This rubric is intended to be an example.

CHAPTER 4

THE IMPORTANCE OF ASSESSMENT

The assessment is one of the most essential elements of school leadership and operation. In today's educational world of accountability, assessment is the tool used to measure schools, teachers, students, and administrator successes. When students are assessed both formative and summative, they should receive feedback immediately. However, assessment is a misunderstood event in the daily operation of the school. Most assessments are not planned or scheduled; the assessments just happen. In many cases, the central office test coordinator working with state departments of education and testing coordinators to schedules the testing, and in many cases, the dates are not aligned with the school's calendar. Teachers do not have sufficient time to teach the content, and in some cases fail to teach all content necessary for student success on the state assessments. The use of pacing guides and curriculum alignment tools aid in the process of transforming a low- performing school into a high-performing one.

The assessment must be defined and clear definable goals of the purpose of the assessment understood by all stakeholders. Students who are taking the SAT should know that they are being compared to a national group of test takers and the purpose of the test is to aid them in gaining college entrance. The test takers should understand the better he or she does on the test increases the chance of gaining college acceptance where he or she desires to go. In like manner, teachers should know how to prepare the students for the SAT by gaining as much knowledge as possible about the content of the test. It makes no sense to teach students content that is not on the test because a teacher feels especially proficient in each content area (hobby teaching). The way I know that teachers are hobby teaching is because they ask for media equipment or films that are outdated and when I walk into their rooms to observe, there are no visual or tactile aids available to the students. This type of teaching does little to help students prepare for any type of assessment.

Reeves (2005) states, "Assessments are the most time-consuming activity for teachers, requiring not only classroom time for administration but many hours of professional time to create and score these assessments. Of all the time-wasting activities in schools, assessments designed exclusively for the evaluation of students with the expectation of improved performance must surely be the most pernicious and disrespectful activities in which we engage. Single assessments scream to students that teacher feedback is irrelevant and that any feedback the students receive is too late to influence performance." With Reeves' view of assessments in mind, neither students nor teachers benefit from assessments that are untimely and fail to provide sufficient feedback. The critical part of assessments is to determine the alignment of the four curricula in a school. Diagram two (on page 24) below demonstrates how the four overshadow each other and the most important part of school improvement lies at the very heart of this alignment.

Assessment and Curriculum Alignment

Leaders in school divisions where I had the pleasure of serving recognized the need for their involvement in setting a dynamic path for school improvement. They were visible in the school and showed an enthusiasm for instruction. These dynamic leaders encouraged me to take chances with change in instructional pedagogy and scheduling to benefit those students who needed additional instructional time. They provided flexibility in working with difficult students whose parents were not involved in their education and teachers who were less than content proficient. I made it my business to learn as much as possible about school improvement and read all articles I could find about curriculum and alignment.

I found that in the schools where I went to work (academically challenged) there was one basic problem, the content taught did not match the content tested (Diagram One Below). The following diagrams provide an overview of the problem from a principal's point of view. I learned that there are four curricula in a school:

1. The **Taught Curriculum**: what the teachers taught the students.
2. The **Learned Curriculum**: what the students learned.
3. The **Written Curriculum**: what the district and school said would be taught to the children.
4. The **External Assessed Curriculum**: what the state used to assess whether all student groups were learning the content necessary to meet the federal government's accepted standards.

Diagram one below illustrates the relationship of these curricula to each other in an unsuccessful school. Diagram two (page 23) illustrates the relationship of these curricula to each other in a high-performing school. Keep in mind this is the one challenge that faces the principals of failing schools, and all leaders in the school must focus on alignment of these curricula to meet the increasing mandates of NCLB.

<u>Diagram One: Curricula Alignment Model of a Poor-Performing School</u>

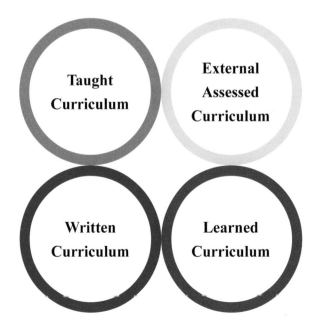

There are four curricula in all schools. The more transposed these curricula are, the higher the academic achievement of the school's students. The illustration to the right is of an academically challenged school.

Diagram Two: Curricula Alignment Model of a High-Performing School

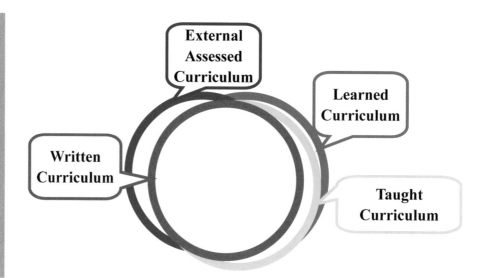

The curricula to the right are of a school that is academically successful and well on its way to full academic success and meeting the accreditation standards according to NCLB.

External Assessed Curriculum

Learned Curriculum

Written Curriculum

Taught Curriculum

Teachers Must Analyze Assessment Results

Data resulting from regular administration of a variety of formative assessments can provide teachers with significant amounts of information about their instructional practices concerning what worked, what did not, and where do I go from here? Neither the formative assessment nor the data need to be extraordinarily displayed but it must be understood. Teachers can compile student responses to find out which students are missing achievement targets and how. Often, patterns or trends will emerge when teachers ask and answer questions, such as "Are all of my students making the same kind of mistakes on the same questions?" "Do their mistakes show that they do not have the ability to synthesize, apply, and/or evaluate the content?" or "Could my students demonstrate understanding if the question format were changed?" Constructing formative assessments so that "in a given set of items, the wrong-answer options reveal specific student misunderstandings" (Popham, 2006, p. 86) can yield precise indicators to guide teacher follow-up instruction. It is critical that teachers provide feedback to student concerning assessment results and discuss areas of improvement.

O'Shea (2005) states that nominal alignment is the way most school districts have responded to the mandates of NCLB. He says that districts have made the mistake of only inserting standards numbers into curriculum guides resulting in little or no change in the way teachers use the materials. As a principal, it is of the utmost importance that teachers understand how to use these guides and related ancillary materials. The curriculum alignment process takes place in departmental meetings where teachers, department chairpersons, and principals make instructional adjustment based on the end of course assessment.

Critical Example of Providing Feedback

I was born in the south with a deep memory of the civil war and segregation that so gripped the social fabric that it was almost impossible to learn of the broader cultural context of the United States. Learning the language of empowerment was overshadowed by the problematic language of blatantly overt and unashamedly racism. The thought of education was not in my mental facilities, but I wondered what constituted learning and how did one learn new things. I also wondered how a person learned further information to become more intelligent or how to build a knowledge base for application when it comes to manipulating one's environment.

Some years later, as I begin to launch out into the deep of life, I learned that those who cared about my development and entrance into the social order always provided feedback concerning the norms in society. So, the critical element to learning and inculcating one's education is feedback from individuals who are highly skilled in work experiences or educational opportunities that one has experienced. The teaching of knowledge always involves results from a set of tasks performed under certain conditions to a (criteria) standard. For example, when I was twelve years old, I learned to plow with a team of mules, and for me to be considered proficient in this activity, I had to plow a straight row for a minimum of thirty feet. My father and older brothers were the highly skilled individuals in this scenario, and they provided coaching as I performed this task.

As a young twelve-year-old, I learned that coaching/feedback is a critical link in learning, and it sparks a learner's curiosity or cultivate their desire for continuous discovery in life. What I did not know about the plowing process was that it prepared the ground for seeds which produced food in later months, the skilled coach could see the end, and I only saw learning the process of plowing. The moving of organic materials to sub-soil as nutrients for the plants' roots was not in my mental picture, but the skilled coach providing the feedback knew what the results would be.

Knowing the results is imperative in learning or sharing experiences. Many educational researchers have written volumes concerning this process; some call it backward planning, and others call it begin with the end in mind. The key to learning is knowing where you want to take your students and be ready to make corrections along the way. Making shifts in the coaching/feedback process always require identifying the data at the center of success; in other words, what constitutes learner or experiment success.

As an adult, one of the major disasters of my life is that of the Challenger. Our astronauts lost their lives willing to learning something new for humanity, but their desire to learn was met with a known possibility of failure. According to the report, "The cause of the Challenger accident was determined to be the failure of O-rings in the right-hand booster joint to contain the pressure of hot gases produced by burning rocket fuel. Flames burned through the booster wall, causing the booster to tear away from the external tank, which ruptured, spilling highly flammable liquid hydrogen and liquid oxygen.

Low temperatures on launch day stiffened the rubber O-rings so much that they could not maintain a seal in a joint that, because of poor design, opened the gap the rings were supposed to seal in the first second after ignition.

Neither NASA nor booster manufacturer Morton Thiokol Inc. understood how the joints worked, nor did they test the joints in a reasonable simulation of how they would be used in flight.

Both NASA and Thiokol were playing "a kind of Russian roulette" by continuing to fly the shuttle despite known problems. They "accepted escalating risk apparently because they 'got away with it last time.'"

Although NASA officials repeatedly told the commission that there was no correlation between cold temperatures and O-ring problems on previous flights, the commission found the opposite and said that NASA should have, too. In all four prior flights that launched below 65 degrees, there was damage to O-rings. By contrast, of 20 flights in warmer weather, only three experienced O-ring damage.

Top NASA officials in Washington received a sufficiently detailed briefing on the O-ring problems in August 1985 to have stopped shuttle flights long enough to correct the problem. But they did not."

The feedback after each flight of the shuttle provided information that failure of the O-Ring was imminent; however, the rush, the hurry, and the push forward caused a breakdown of the team to make mid-stream corrections. The educational process requires mid-stream corrections when the feedback from classroom assessment data, other formative assessment data, and overall student grades data says failure is imminent. As educators, we can use the Challenger example to move our students forward academically when data informs us those changes in instructional practices are needed.

Giving students timely feedback on formative assessments along with coaching is a critical step in the learner's success. The feedback to students should also be viewed as a teacher allocated instructional action during a class period. In other words, no assessment should be given without time planned in the schedule for students' individual and collective feedback. Teachers should make sure the feedback addresses the objective and provides multiple opportunities for students to revise their work to broaden and deepen the understanding of the topic. I recommend the use of the RISE Model by Emily Wray (file:///C:/Users/Thomas/Documents/RISE_rubric-peer.pdf). In her model she provides an excellent framework for giving students peer to peer feedback and this tool can be used by teachers to provide feedback as well.

At this point, I need to talk about parent teacher conferences. The gathering of student data provides teachers with background information to paint a picture of a student's academic success or the lack thereof. I also found that most teacher lack the experience necessary to conduct an effective parent teacher conference. Therefore, while I was the principal of Antilles High School, we developed a tip sheet for teacher actions prior to and after the conference, see below.

Parent-Teacher Conference

Parent teacher conferences are an important aspect of on-going home and school communication involving family engagement. Many years of research have concluded that family involvement in education can lead to positive benefits for students and teachers alike. Teachers become more aware of the aspiration's parents have for their children academically and teachers become more aware of their own teaching practices. Students gain a greater appreciation of the preparation and sacrifice teachers make to the profession of education. As the principal of Antilles High School (AHS), my purpose for this tip sheet is to help teacher facilitate parent-teacher conferences in a manner where the conference reaches its maximum potential. The tip sheet will offer some suggestions that will assist and support teachers as they prepare, conduct, and follow-up with parents after the conference.

Pre-conference:

1. Communicate with parents and stress the importance of the conference
   - Send a reminder email or phone call to parents to ensure the date and time of the conference
   - If the child has an IEP be sure to get the document and reread it to ensure that you are meeting the accommodations.
   - Get a statement of the student's behavior from other teachers who teach him or her
   - Get current graders from your class and other teachers not just grade speed but current grades.
   - Get student behavior reports from other classes and attendance clerk
   - Get a copy of the student's schedule
   - Get copies of student work that is well done and that which is not so well done
   - Organize the materials so as to paint a picture of the student you are teaching.

- Prepare notes for the conference always start the conference with a positive note or statement about the student.
- If you are expecting difficult parents, then you should rehearse your conference with a colleague until you feel comfortable. A good rehearsal build confidence.
- Hold the conference in an inviting area and make sure that you have student data available in an explainable format.

2. Make sure to double check everything and remember being well organized demonstrates that you know the child as an individual, this is your last item before the conference day.

Conference:

1. Discuss progress and growth
   - Greet parents and thank them for coming in to see you concerning their child
   - Start with a positive statement
   - Let family know about their child's ability in the content area in relationship to his or her peers
   - Help parents understand academic or behavior data
   - Demonstrate student progress against learning goals
   - Identify the area that need to be addressed

2. Use examples
   - Walk parents through an assignment and assessments to provide clarity and point out where students did not demonstrate mastery of the content
   - Ask if they have any questions that you might be able to answer
   - Solicit input from the parents concerning the student's strengths and areas of needed improvement, suggest that you are working with them as a team for their child's academic success.

- Ask parents about their hopes and dreams for their child and how you can help them reach those goals
- Suggest ideas and strategies that parents can use at home to help their child grow and always be an active listener

3. Seek solution collaboratively with parents
   - Avoid judgment of the child, like, your child needs to study more, or he or she needs to do homework.
   - State, how can we work together to ensure that your child is successful?
   - How can we work together to resolve this problem?

4. Make an action plan
   - Spend the last few minutes of your time discussing how you and the family can work together to support the student.
   - Be specific about the kinds of things you will do, how long you will do them and how often you will check with the family concerning the student's progress
   - Establish lines of communication by what means i.e., email, phone calls, letters, and student agenda and so on.
   - Establish a way to follow-up on your conference in the next two weeks

5. Post conference
   - Follow-up with family with a thank you note for their help in making sure that their child was successful academically
   - Ask if they have any questions concerning the conference
   - Agree to stay connected on a regular basis
   - Close the conference by making parents aware of other opportunities for them to be involved in the school by providing them with a school monthly calendar

6. As the principal, I stand with you in support of your efforts to make the students at AHS successful academically, socially, and emotionally. I am also available to be in the conference with you when you meet with parents.

CHAPTER 5

HOLDING STAFF ACCOUNTABLE FOR HIGH EXPECTATIONS

There are several important requirements in today's educational arena; however, none is as important as setting high expectations and holding those responsible for delivery of education services accountable for student academic success. In the schools and districts where academic success by all groups of students is realized, leadership and high expectations are key factors. Principals, central office administrators, and superintendents hold all persons in the delivery of instructional services responsible. In the schools where I served as principal, I held teachers responsible for setting high expectations according to standards set in High Schools That Work (HSTW), Virginia Standards of Learning (SOL), and No Child Left Behind (NCLB) for meeting AYP. In addition, I held teachers accountable for **data** collection for the purpose of alignment of the four curricula in the school.

As described in the preceding chapter, assessment and teacher understanding of this evaluation approach is critical in school accreditation. The national, state, district, and school assessment has taken on new meaning, with the goal of meeting several purposes: monitoring student progress; holding schools and teachers accountable for student performance; certifying student achievement and skills; aligning curriculum, instruction, and grading; and influencing instructional practices.

Data collected during the instructional process should reveal that teachers understand several factors that function as barriers in the assessment of students in their classroom. Teachers are to act, as facilitators of instruction should work intensely to overcome the barriers to achieving the stated purposes of performance assessment systems. For example, if a state develops and implements an assessment system based on technology for certifying student achievement, then a procedure for collection of student assessment **data** is the responsibility of the teacher and should be monitored by the principal for the intended use of the system and remediation. Most states have a reporting system, which very few teachers can access. These two examples represent two barriers to using the state technology system to measure student achievement; no system that is technologically unsound or not user friendly can be justifiably used for measuring student academic capabilities.

The one ill-refutable purpose the state **data** collection system serves is to provide opportunity for a longitudinal analysis of teacher quality as it relates to student academic achievement. I was able to use Virginia's **data** disaggregator to review teacher **data** from the previous four years. I used that information to assign teachers according to the needs of students. To the students who were the neediest, I assigned the more proficient teachers, based on their assessment score from the state tracking system. The teachers who had advanced degrees were assigned Advanced Placement (AP) and dual enrollment courses because of the local community college requirements. Teachers, who demonstrated low student academic achievement over prolonged periods were placed on assistance plans and moved to teaching developmental courses, and in some cases, were asked to find employment in another profession. Without an excellent student performance data collection tool, it would be impossible to move a school to full accreditation. The following is a tool, which was used to assist teachers and department chairpersons in developing a curriculum, alignment, instruction, and data-monitoring tool. This tool is one approach to holding stakeholders responsible for essential actions at a given point in the school year.

Curriculum, Alignment, Instruction, Data Monitoring, and Responsibility Tool

This tool is used for monitoring data feedback from all four curricula by the superintendent, principal, teachers, and students, with emphasis on expected outcomes. The result of using such a tool would bring the four curricula in the school closer together, and in some cases the curricula would be completely aligned (superimposed or one circle) (Diagram three on page 22).

Superintendent's Essential Actions	Principal's Essential Actions	Teachers' Essential Actions	Timeline
1. Review each school's data once every month, looking for trends and asking relevant questions. Set benchmark percentage pass rate for students.	Review teacher data weekly or bi-weekly, asking department chairpersons and teachers relevant questions about negative or positive trends. Summer workshop on data collection, standards-based instruction, and development of data collection tool.	Review and disaggregate assessment data weekly and compile a data book of all taught objectives. Maintain data on all students who did not meet school standards. Also, maintain records of students' remediation and their success percentage.	June or July time frame; no later than thirty instructional days into the school year or as early as possible.
2. Ask questions about staff development for teachers who are not meeting, the districts benchmark standard.	Review the data of staff members who are on assistance plans and provide staff development in areas of low student academic performance. Brief superintendent of bi-weekly assessment data.	Review assessment results with students and schedule student remediation as needed. Brief principal and department chairpersons on bi-weekly assessment data	Ten instructional days into school or as early as possible.
3. Set aside resources for staff development and remediation during the day	Coordinate remediation for students who need the service after school, early morning, and double block schedule for students who are in danger of being unsuccessful. Identify teachers who need additional classroom management assistance and help with data analysis. Provide data workshops for department chairpersons	Department chairpersons provide data assistance workshops under the guidance of the principal.	Fifteen instructional days into the school year or as soon as possible.

Superintendent's Essential Actions	Principal's Essential Actions	Teachers' Essential Actions	Timeline
4. Identify and place principals on assistance plan who need this type of help.	Identify essential actions to be corrected and collaboratively with superintendent establish corrective action timeline. Establish an evaluation plan for teachers on data analysis. Remove department chairpersons who are unwilling to take the leadership initiative in the data workshop process.	Establish a data analysis plan and departmental meeting schedule with assistance of department chairperson.	June or July during summer work schedule
5. Principal report on first six- or nine-week's data.	Review first six- or nine-weeks data and brief the superintendent	Review first six- or nine-week's data and brief department chairpersons and principal	End of the first six or nine weeks

This tool is not an end all to **data** monitoring; however, it does provide leaders at each level of the school division's bureaucracy with a timeline and responsibility chart for data. Principals, data is the engine that drives your school and the more you know and understand student, teacher, and community behavior from a data perspective, the better you can lead your school.

Data Collection

Collection of **data** is a problem for most leaders. In most schools the task of **data** analysis and collection are functions given to a teacher or groups of teachers. This is one of the most critical and fatal mistakes of a new, or in some cases, seasoned principal. **Data** collection and analysis are the most important aspects of school operation in a standards-based environment. How can one-change directions if he or she does not have reference point? **Data** collection and analysis provides that reference point.

On page 26 is one example of a **data** collection tool. This tool is a variation of a **data** tool developed and used by Richmond City Public Schools.

As a principal, I wanted the responsibility of collecting and analyzing the school's **data**. This decision proved to be the most important leadership decision I made. I understood my biases; therefore, I would look at the **data** for positive and negative trends. In many school systems that are failing, leaders have risen through the ranks and have not experienced success at any level. It is difficult for those types of leaders to see data from various experiences. The leader who has always been in one school division that has not experienced academic success will only have failing experiences from which to make decisions. Holcomb (2000) provides a flow chart with a few questions concerning **data**. One of the questions is "Where are we now?" The question begs for an answer; however, without the knowledge of the school's mission and the **data** collected from previous assessments, student discipline, student, and teacher attendance, and so on, one cannot answer this basic question.

The information collected should provide the analyst with a portfolio of the school. According to Holcomb, the portfolio should lead to additional questions and concerns when the principal or other administrative leaders ask the question, "Where do we want to go?" There are priority goals that need to be established and a collection of research information concerning these goals. There are three additional questions Holcomb proposes. The first question is "How will we get there?" This question can be answered by the selection of research-based teaching strategies. The second question is "How will we know we are getting there?" The indicators answer this question from student achievement, attendance, discipline, parental involvement, and graduation rate **data**, just to name a few. The third question is "How will we get there?" This question is relating to the action plan. The answer to this question is with actions plan to address each indicator. Holcomb finishes the discussion by addressing sustaining focus and momentum by development of a master plan. There is an example of a master plan in Appendix A. This plan is used by the state of Virginia to address the academic areas in schools that have not met state standards in several consecutive years.

Diagram Three: A School Where the Curriculum is Completely Aligned

The circles to the right represent a school where the curricula are completely aligned

External Assessed Curriculum

Learned Curriculum

Written Curriculum

Taught Curriculum

Data Collection Tool

Principal: <u>XXX</u>   Bi-Weekly Report

School: <u>   </u>   Quarterly Report

Date:

Assessments	Total # of Students Tested	# Scoring 60% & Below	%	# Scoring 61-79%	%	# Scoring 80% and Above	%
Earth Science I			#DIV/0!		#DIV/0!		#DIV/0!
			#DIV/0!		#DIV/0!		#DIV/0!

Assessments	Total # of Students Tested	# Scoring 60% & Below	%	# Scoring 61-79%	%	# Scoring 80% and Above	%
Earth Science II			#DIV/0!		#DIV/0!		#DIV/0!
			#DIV/0!		#DIV/0!		#DIV/0!
			#DIV/0!		#DIV/0!		#DIV/0!

Assessments	Total # of Students Tested	# Scoring 60% & Below	%	# Scoring 61-79%	%	# Scoring 80% and Above	%
Biology I							

Assessments	Total # of Students Tested	# Scoring 60% & Below	%	# Scoring 61-79%	%	# Scoring 80% and Above	%
Biology II							

Assessments	Total # of Students Tested	# Scoring 60% & Below	%	# Scoring 61-79%	%	# Scoring 80% and Above	%
Chemistry							

Subject Totals	Total # of Students Tested	# Scoring 60% & Below	%	# Scoring 61-79%	%	# Scoring 80% and Above	%
			#DIV/0!		#DIV/0!		#DIV/0!
			#DIV/0!		#DIV/0!		#DIV/0!
			#DIV/0!		#DIV/0!		#DIV/0!
			#DIV/0!		#DIV/0!		#DIV/0!
			#DIV/0!		#DIV/0!		#DIV/0!
			#DIV/0!		#DIV/0!		#DIV/0!

CHAPTER 6

THE INSTRUCTIONAL PROCESS

The instructional dynamics that take place in the classroom today is a complex and a misunderstood process. There are many books written attempting to explain what takes place in an increasingly diverse instructional setting. As a principal of both middle and high schools, I found this to be one of my greatest challenges. All the literature written did not prepare me for the challenge. Once a teacher closes his or her door only the students and teacher know what takes place behind the closed door.

There are several factors that affect learning, however, the one major factor primarily, that affects student academic success is the teacher student relationship. In this chapter, I will discuss the components in the instructional model list below.

The Instructional Model

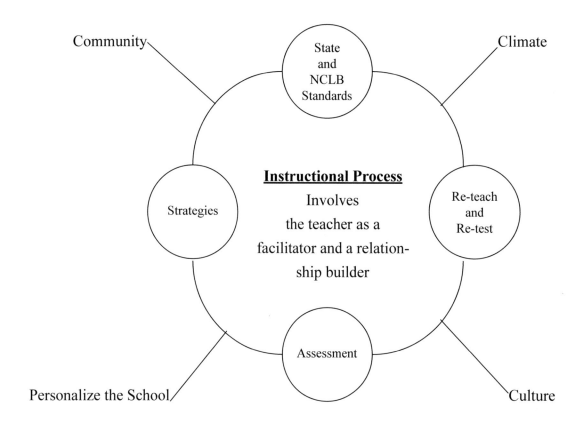

The model is not all-inclusive; however, it represents what was used in each of the schools where I served as principal. The circles represent actions taken in the classroom by the teacher/facilitator and the words outside of the circle represent external forces influencing the school and classroom-learning environment.

The one major question asked by each principal I talked with is "What should students know and be able to do at the end of teacher-conducted instruction?" My answer is always "What is the standard asking the student to accomplish?" Rutherford (2002) states the first thing to consider when teaching in a standards-based environment is "What should students know and be able to do?" In Virginia and most other states, the first thing students should be able to accomplish are tasks to the state standards and teachers and principals should know that the school must accomplish this to the standards of NCLB.

The second question Rutherford deals with is "How will I, and they, know when they are successful?" This question is from a teacher's perspective. The teacher is the first one to know if a student is successful. The teacher knows the student response to the teaching strategies. The dynamics involving the teacher as a facilitator will provide enough feedback for the teacher and student to know if he or she is successful. The assessment is the tool teachers use to evaluate their instruction and serves as a form of accountability for the teacher. The teacher uses research-based teaching practices to facilitate student academic success. The fourth part to this teaching paradigm is test data. The test data is not the external test data, but teacher made test data. Teachers should re-teach those students whose data indicates they are not successful.

External Forces Impacting the Learning Environment

There are many community practices that affect the school-learning environment. In urban schools, the gang happening on the past evening, the dating and other gang-related activities has a profound impact on the local schools. One of the most important ways to overcome these types of instructional distractions is to make sure students cannot remain anonymous for four years in a high school (Breaking Ranks II 2004). Principals must ensure that all students are involved in some type of school related activity. This provides the student with a sense of belonging to the larger community, and it personalizes the school environment.

While I was serving as principal in one urban high school, we developed a program called the High Incentive Performance Program (HIPP) to influence the school-learning environment. The program focused on student attendance, academics, and behavior because **data** indicated that these were major problem areas. Grade-level principals would encourage their students to ensure that all their friends attended school and completed their assignments. We offered rewards for the grade level that had the best attendance for the grading period or the grade level that had the best grade point average (GPA) for the grading period. We offered rewards for the grade level that had fewer disciplinary infractions for a grading period. That one program was responsible for decreasing our disciplinary incidents over the previous year by twenty-five percent.

The HIPP program also allowed the faculty, community, and businesses to become involved with the change in climate throughout the building and community. The culture changed when we told students they could have a dance or some other school-related activity. They expected that activity to happen and they took responsibility for policing their fellow students to ensure no discipline issues would prevent the activity. The primary focus of the program was to provide students with opportunities they had not experienced to that point in their educational matriculation. Teachers who needed additional assistance with content and pedagogical development were given the assistance during the summer. There is a budget for a summer staff development workshop in Appendix A.

The last point of interest in the above diagram is the relationship between the teacher and student. The classroom is a place of ever-changing dynamics. The learners and the teachers are exploring new avenues of possibilities. The learners push the envelope of teacher knowledge to forge new experiences, creating new knowledge. The teachers' use of activities and related life experiences to demand deeper syntheses of the knowledge acquired by the learners is a critical part of education. This dynamic is education. The use of one's education is the demand of the social order in solving everyday problems, which brings about the discovery of new cures for various diseases that plague society. One who has a good education, applies the knowledge gained to analyze truth from fiction and exaggeration. An educated person uses his or her education to develop a broader world understanding of global warming and future changes in our environment. Education is for the betterment of society, and those who uses their education to this end are forever memorialized by history.

Principals, you have an awesome task. You must not lose focus of the process of teaching and learning on the part of your faculty and student body. The future demands it. This short book is my effort to assist those who toil day in and day out with the hope of accomplishing the task of public-school accreditation.

As I pondered the question of who would read this book, I consider the sobering thought that every principal will read it and gain some new perspective on leadership. I want to leave you with one last word from Reverend Doctor Martin Luther King. "People will work together and sacrifice if they understand clearly why and how the sacrifice will bring about change. Never assume that anyone understands. It is your job to keep people informed and aware.

As a principal of six high schools, I was never an advocate of students doing extra credit to get a better grade. Remember, teaching is not for a grade but learning the content and a grade is assigned for content mastery. Assignments and formative assessments in the classroom allow a student to demonstrate mastery and if a teacher assigns additional work in an area, it should be for enrichment. I should say something here about make up work, students should complete assignments when they are due. The student can get assistance with the content at that point and learning of the content can be assured by the teacher. To allow students to just make up an assignment at the end of the semester when content mastery has not been established for a grade is a total waste of time and effort. The student takes the external assessment where content mastery is required but he or she fails because content mastery was never established.

CHAPTER 7

DEVELOPING BUILDING LEADERSHIP

I have not spoken much about my personal desires for leadership or the various styles of leadership, except for Douglas Reeves discussion of leadership maps. I would be remised if I did not discuss educational leadership from a building principal's perspective. Much of my seventy-three years of life have been lived out in a few leadership positions. I was a nineteen-year-old Infantry squad leader in the Republic of Vietnam, a twenty-three-year old platoon sergeant in an Armor Battalion in the Federal Republic of Germany, a thirty-two-year old first sergeant of a tank company in Fort Knox, Kentucky and Germany, a thirty-nine-year old Sergeants Major of a Calvary Squadron in Fort Lewis, Washington, a pastor of two Baptist churches, and into the principalship of two middle schools and seven high schools; my life has been filled with leadership.

After fifty-four years of experience in leadership, I think there are a few things I can add to the community of knowledge as it relates to leadership. In all organizations, there is a formal and informal leadership chain. The principal that wishes to be successful at turning around a school academically must recognize this fact and be prepared to work within that framework for one to two years. The informal leader has the ear of the higher-level authorities most of the time, the conversation is negative. No higher-level leader wants to hear negative information and they would move the principal rath than deal with negativity.

As I stated earlier, leadership is expressed as an art form. However, it can only be an art form once an individual fully understands and embodies the art. In the Army Field Manual 22-100, leadership is expressed as the process of influencing others to accomplish the mission by providing purpose, direction, and motivation. Upon assuming the responsibility of a school as a principal, the new leader must determine what is expected of the faculty, students, and staff. The new leader must determine what is expected of him or her. By using historical and current data, the new principal must determine the strengths and weaknesses of all staff, faculty, and other stakeholders. The final part of the new leader assessment is to determine who are the other key personnel that will play a key role in the success of the school, students, and seek the support of those persons.

Development of Leaders

In the position of principal, you have some authority; however, the authority is only realized in an autocratic organization. In a democratic organization, a principal gets his or her authority from school board regulations and policies, department of education memos, and state department of education superintendent's memos. The principal because of the nature of the office is the building leader. In the office, the principal must set a good example for the followers to emulate. One of the major shortcomings of most principals is failure to develop young leaders in the building where he or she serves.

Leadership development at the building level is essential for sustaining momentum in school improvement. Development of teacher leaders is important because it allows young teachers to take part in the building-level vision, and it builds leadership capacity in the throughout the school building. The faculty feels empowered when they have a role in decision making and see that students are successful. A wise principal develops a leadership program for teachers and assistant principals. After the training is completed, the principal provides leadership opportunities such as organizing graduation, providing oversight of the prom, and organizing and conducting parent-teacher conferences or school open houses. I used these activities to introduce teachers to the backward planning process and brainstorming activity. Principals, I would suggest that you establish a suspense file to keep track of all building and central office suspenses and make notes on who you assigned a certain activity. Once you have assigned the suspense, coach the faculty member to ensure that the assignment reaches completion but also to encourage the teacher, become the teacher's cheerleader.

As the principal, you should conduct a task analysis of the difficult tasks that are assigned to you. You can accomplish several difficult tasks when you assign the tasks to teacher leaders who may be gifted in that area. Develop teacher ownership of the school and, support the teachers when they make a difficult decision with less than desirable results. Take that opportunity to teach the teacher leaders with patience, understanding, and direction. You win their support and dedication when you provide the same support and dedication. I sincerely hope your tenure as principal goes well and your school reaches accreditation.

Appendix (A)

Remediation Record Instrument (Example).

Name of Student	Objective Tested	Date of Remediation	Date of Re-test
1. Doe, John	A1 (Algebra I)	Nov. 15, 2006	Nov. 17, 2006
2.			
3			

Appendix (A)

Proposed Budget for Teacher Summer Curriculum Work 2006 (Example).

Plan: each of the four core curriculum areas will work within their departments as a team to:
- Build on work begun in 2005-06 to raise student achievement on SOL test measures
- Develop instructional strategies and common assessments to monitor student progress on each SOL objective throughout the course
- Provide professional development through working together on common departmental and school needs

- Incorporate the pacing/alignment and monitoring processes into departmental plans for 2006-07.

There will be one consultant hired to train teachers in good test preparation at the beginning of the session. In addition, test banks of SOL-like test items will be purchased for teacher use during their work sessions. It is also possible that at least one or more consultant teachers for each core area will be hired from outside the district to advise each core area.

Time frame:
1. **July or August: 7 days, 5 hours per day except English**
2. **August: English: 4 days for one week, 5 hours per day**
3. **August: one day for 6 hours for each core department including all teachers to review plans made, review pacing guides for each subject area, and prepare monitoring process to begin first day of school.**

Budget: $25 p/hour p/teacher + $200 p/day for each curriculum specialist + funds to prepare final written copy.

Mathematics:

- 12 teachers x $25 p/hr x 5 hrs p/day x 7 days $10,500
- 1 curriculum Specialist x $200 p/day $ 1,400
- 1 consultant teacher x $200 p/day $ 1,400
- Written preparation of material: $200 x 3 teachers $ 600

                  TOTAL   **$ 13,900**

Science

- 9 teachers x $25 p/hr x 5 hrs p/day x 7 days $ 7,875
- 1 Curriculum Specialist x $200 p/day $ 1,400
- 1 consultant teacher x $200 p/day $ 1,400
- Written preparation of material: $200 x 3 teachers $ 600

                 TOTAL   **$ 11,275**

Social Studies

- 11 teachers x $25 p/hr. x 5 hrs. p/day x 7 days $ 9,625
- 1 Curriculum Specialist x$200p/day $ 1,400
- 1 consultant teacher x $200 p/day $ 1,400
- Written preparation of material: $200 x 3 teachers $ 600

                 TOTAL   **$13,025**

English

- 6 teachers x $25 p/hr. x 5 hrs. p/day x 4 days $ 3,000
- 1 Curriculum Specialist x $200 p/day $ 800
- 1 consultant teacher x $200 p/day $ 800
- Written preparation of material: $200 x 3 teachers $ 600

TOTAL   **$ 5,200**

August review day

- 44 teachers x $25 p/hr. x 6 hrs.   **$ 6,600**

GRAND TOTAL   **$50,000**

Additional expenses:

Trainer for first day   **$ 2,000**

Three-Year School Improvement Plan

A Description of How the School will Meet the Provisional Accreditation Benchmarks, or
the Requirements to be Fully Accredited, for Each of the Years Covered by the Plan
(8 VAC 20-131-310.G.1)

School-wide Goal: **By the end of 2005-2006 school year, 85% of (Blank School) students will pass all SOL tests required.**

Goal Statement: **By the end of 2005-2006 school year, 70% of the Biology students will pass the Biology SOL test.**

Objective: **By the end of 2005-2006, 70% of the students will have a proficiency score of at least 30 in Biology in all reporting categories:**

Category 1 – to maintain at 30 or increase the scale score in "Scientific investigation" to above 30.

Category 2 –to maintain at 30 or increase the scale score in "Life at the Molecular & Cellular Level" to above 30.

Category 3 – to maintain at 30 or increase the scale score in "Life at the Systems & Organisms Level" to above 30.

Category 4 – to increase the scale score in "Interaction of Life Forms" to or above 30.

Specific measures of student achievement that will be taken throughout the school year(s)
and used to monitor academic improvement over time (8 VAC 20 – 131-310.G.2):

Types of Assessments	Frequency of Measures and Data Collection	Evidence/Data to be Collected
Teacher prepared ten monthly unit tests in SOL format.	Ten-unit tests given once each month from September 2005 through June 2006.	Grade book and tracking sheets that record the data analysis of assessments.
Teacher prepared quizzes given on a weekly basis in SOL format.	Weekly quizzes beginning with September 2, 2005	Grade book record of quiz scores on weekly checkpoints
Team of Biology teachers to prepare and administer common nine weeks test and semester examinations to benchmark student progress.	October 30 through November 1 – 4, 2005; the week of January 22 – 27, 2005; April 1 – 3, 2006.	Grade book, tracking sheets and report cards.

ADD ROWS AS NEEDED TO ACCOMMODATE NUMBER OF ASSESSMENT TOOLS

Strategies and/or Action Steps	8 VAC 20-131-310 Code (place **x** by all that apply)	Projected Time Frame	**Person (s)** Responsible	**Financial Resources Needed (estimate amount and cite sources) G.9**	Other Resources Needed	Evidence of Implementation of the Strategy	**OCTOBER 1 STATUS** (If not implemented according to projected time frame, provide explanation.)
GENERAL STRATEGIES FOR ALL SCIENCE SUBJECTS	██████	██████	██████	██████	██████	██████	
STRATEGY 1 - Teachers will collaborate to develop 9 weeks benchmark assessment tests to be given at least three times during the school year. Questions on the test will be grouped according to reporting categories.	☐G.4 ☒G.5 ☐G.6 ☐G.7	Beginning September 2, 2005 through end of third 9 weeks period. (April 1, 2006)	Biology Teachers	none	Cracking the VA SOLs Curriculum Framework Curriculum Guide Released TAAS Flanagan test	Grade book Administrative Observation Pacing Guides Tracking Sheets	

Strategies and/or Action Steps	8 VAC 20-131-310 Code (place **x** by all that apply)	Projected Time Frame	**Person (s)** Responsible	**Financial Resources Needed (estimate amount and cite sources) G.9**	Other Resources Needed	Evidence of Implementation of the Strategy	**OCTOBER 1 STATUS** (If not implemented according to projected time frame, provide explanation.)
Action Step #1: By September 30, 50% of the questions will be written for the first 9 weeks benchmark test.	☐G.4 ☒G.5 ☐G.6 ☐G.7	Beginning September 2, 2005 through June 11, 2006.	Biology Teachers	none	Cracking the VA SOLs Flanagan Test Released TAAS Curriculum Guide Curriculum Framework	Grade Book Tracking Sheets Administrative Observations Pacing Guide Tracking Sheets	
STRATEGY 2: Continue last years' Extended Day Program for Remediation Weekly. (Monday – Thursday)*	☒G.4 ☐G.5 ☐G.6 ☐G.7	Beginning September 15, 2005 through April 1, 2006.	SOL Subject Teachers Assistant Principal in charge	Approximately $170,000	Classroom resources already being used by subject area teachers	Weekly Student Rosters	
Action Step # 1: Select the teachers who will do Remediation instruction.	☒G.4 ☐G.5 ☐G.6 ☐G.7	September 8-12, 2005	Assistant Principal	none	none	Letters to parents Schedule/ Permission Form for Extended Day Classes Administrative Observations	

Strategies and/or Action Steps	8 VAC 20-131-310 Code (place **x** by all that apply)	Projected Time Frame	**Person (s)** Responsible	**Financial Resources Needed (estimate amount and cite sources) G.9**	Other Resources Needed	Evidence of Implementation of the Strategy	**OCTOBER 1 STATUS** (If not implemented according to projected time frame, provide explanation.)
Action Step #2: Teachers identify students who have not scored at least 80% on their class quizzes and tests to attend "Extended Day Program for Remediation".	☒G.4 ☐G.5 ☐G.6 ☐G.7	September 15, 2005 through April 1, 2006. (weekly)	SOL Subject Teachers	Included in overall cost	none	Letters to parents Schedule/ Permission Form for Extended Day classes Administrative Observations	
Action Step #3: Teachers selected for "Extended Day Program for Remediation" and classroom teachers agree on what will be included in instruction.	☒G.4 ☐G.5 ☐G.6 ☐G.7	Beginning weekly September 15, 2005 through April 1, 2006	Biology Teachers Principal Assistant Principal	Included in overall cost o	none	Letters to parents Schedule/ Permission Form for Extended Day Classes Administrative Observations	
Action Step #4: Teachers for "Extended Day Program for Remediation" retest students who received remediation..	☒G.4 ☐G.5 ☐G.6 ☐G.7	Beginning weekly September 15, 2005 through April 1, 2006	Teachers Principal Assistant Principal	Included in overall cost.	none	Letters to parents Schedule/ Permission Form for Extended Day Classes Administrative Observations	

Strategies and/or Action Steps	8 VAC 20-131-310 Code (place **x** by all that apply)	Projected Time Frame	**Person (s)** Responsible	**Financial Resources Needed (estimate amount and cite sources) G.9**	Other Resources Needed	Evidence of Implementation of the Strategy	**OCTOBER 1 STATUS** (If not implemented according to projected time frame, provide explanation.)
STRATEGY 3: At the beginning of each nine weeks, subject area teachers will identify key SOL concepts to display on the walls in the hallway.*	☐G.4 ☒G.5 ☐G.6 ☐G.7	1st 9 Weeks-By October 2, 2005 2nd 9 Weeks – By December 9, 2005 3rd 9 Weeks-By February 27	All Science Teachers	none	Poster Board Magic Markers	Can be observed in the hallway each nine weeks	
Action Step #1: Department chairperson will meet with science teachers to determine how the SOL concepts will be generated.	☐G.4 ☒G.5 ☐G.6 ☐G.7	1st Week of School for Teachers - August 25, 28, 29, 2005	Science Department Chairperson All Science Teachers	none	none	Can be observed in the hallway each nine weeks	
Action Step #2: Concepts will be given to the department chairperson 2 weeks prior to the date the display is to be completed.	☐G.4 ☒G.5 ☐G.6 ☐G.7	1st 9 Weeks – September 18, 2005 2nd o Weeks – November 24, 2005 3rd 9 Weeks – February 13, 2006	All Science Teachers Science Department Chairperson	none	none	Can be observed in the hallway each nine weeks	

Strategies and/or Action Steps	8 VAC 20-131-310 Code (place **x** by all that apply)	Projected Time Frame	**Person (s)** Responsible	**Financial Resources Needed (estimate amount and cite sources) G.9**	Other Resources Needed	Evidence of Implementation of the Strategy	**OCTOBER 1 STATUS** (If not implemented according to projected time frame, provide explanation.)
Action Step #3: Teachers will call students' attention to the displays as a means of continued exposure to what is being taught.	☐G.4 ☒G.5 ☐G.6 ☐G.7	October 2, 2005 – April 1, 2006	All Science Teachers	none	none	Can be observed in the hallway each nine weeks	
STRATEGY 4: Teachers will begin implementing the Chesapeake/ Petersburg Curriculum during the 2003-04 school year.	☐G.4 ☐G.5 ☒G.6 ☐G.7	August 25, 2005 – June 11, 2006	Instructional Specialist for Science All Science Teachers	none	none	Teacher;s Lesson Plans	
Action Step #1: Instructional Specialists will coordinate the workshop(s) for implementation.	☐G.4 ☐G.5 ☒G.6 ☐G.7	August 25, 2005 – April 1, 2006	Science Curriculum Specialist Science Teachers	none	Chesapeake/ Petersburg Curriculum Guides Consulting Help from Chesapeake	Menu for Opening of School Staff Development	

Strategies and/or Action Steps	8 VAC 20-131-310 Code (place **x** by all that apply)	Projected Time Frame	**Person (s)** Responsible	**Financial Resources Needed (estimate amount and cite sources) G.9**	Other Resources Needed	Evidence of Implementation of the Strategy	**OCTOBER 1 STATUS** (If not implemented according to projected time frame, provide explanation.)
Action Step #2: Teachers collaborate to evaluate the alignment of current resources and activities with DOE Curriculum Frameworks and assessments.	☐G.4 ☐G.5 ☒G.6 ☐G.7	August 25, 2005 – April 1, 2006	Science Curriculum Specialist Science Teachers And Department Chairperson	none	Chesapeake/ Petersburg Curriculum Guides Consulting Help from Chesapeake	PHS Monthly Calendar	
Action Step #3: Teachers evaluate the effectiveness of the implementation of the Chesapeake/ Petersburg Curriculum.	☐G.4 ☐G.5 ☒G.6 ☐G.7	April 1, 2006 or thereafter.	Biology Teachers Science Department Chairperson	none	Chesapeake/ Petersburg Curriculum Guides Consulting Help from Chesapeake	PHS Monthly Calendar	
STRATEGY 5: Teachers will turn in lesson plans weekly using the Division Lesson Plans implemented last school year (2002-03).*	☐G.4 ☒G.5 ☐G.6 ☐G.7	September 2, 2005 – June 4, 2006.	Science Department Chairperson Biology Teachers	none	Curriculum Guide Data Disaggregator	Records maintained by Administrators and Department Chairpersons	

Strategies and/or Action Steps	8 VAC 20-131-310 Code (place **x** by all that apply)	Projected Time Frame	**Person (s)** Responsible	**Financial Resources Needed (estimate amount and cite sources) G.9**	Other Resources Needed	Evidence of Implementation of the Strategy	**OCTOBER 1 STATUS** (If not implemented according to projected time frame, provide explanation.)
Action Step #1: Department chairperson will conduct a meeting to inform teachers of how the Division Lesson Plans are to be used.	☐G.4 ☒G.5 ☐G.6 ☐G.7	During the first week of school for teachers: August 25, 26, or 29	Science Department Chairperson Biology Teachers	none	Curriculum Guide Data Disaggregator	Menu for Staff Development for School Opening	
Action Step #2: Subject Area teachers should meet weekly to decide what will be included on lesson plans weekly. (Teachers in each subject area will agree on the day)	☐G.4 ☒G.5 ☐G.6 ☐G.7	Weekly for the remainder of the year-beginning week of September 2	Science Teachers	none	Lesson plan forms Curriculum Guides Data Disaggregator	Plans filed with Assistant Principal	
Action Step #3: Lesson plans should be done in triplicate: 1 for the teacher, 1 for the Assistant Principle, and one for the Department Chairperson.	☐G.4 ☒G.5 ☐G.6 ☐G.7	September 2, 2005 – June 4, 2006	Science Department Chairperson All Science Teachers Assistant Principal	none	none	none	

Strategies and/or Action Steps	8 VAC 20-131-310 Code (place **x** by all that apply)	Projected Time Frame	**Person (s)** Responsible	**Financial Resources Needed (estimate amount and cite sources) G.9**	Other Resources Needed	Evidence of Implementation of the Strategy	**OCTOBER 1 STATUS** (If not implemented according to projected time frame, provide explanation.)
Action Step #4: Current Lesson plans should be displayed in the classroom at all times.	☐G.4 ☒G.5 ☐G.6 ☐G.7	Beginning September 2, 2005– June 11, 2006	All Science Teachers	none	none	Observations of Administrators	
STRATEGY 6: The Chemical Storage Area, work areas between each classroom, and each classroom will be inventoried by the teachers responsible for those areas to provide all teachers with a listing of the materials available for instruction.	☐G.4 ☒G.5 ☐G.6 ☐G.7	September 2, 2005 – September 30, 2005	Science Teachers in the following areas: E201, E202, E203, E204, E205, E213, E214, E215, E216 Teachers are responsible for the areas between two classrooms	none	none	Copies of inventories distributed to each teacher	
Action Step #1: Teachers will place similar items together and count.	☐G.4 ☒G.5 ☐G.6 ☐G.7	September 3, 2005 – September 5, 2005	Science Teachers as indicated above.	none	none	Observations of administrators	

Strategies and/or Action Steps	8 VAC 20-131-310 Code (place **x** by all that apply)	Projected Time Frame	**Person (s)** Responsible	**Financial Resources Needed (estimate amount and cite sources) G.9**	Other Resources Needed	Evidence of Implementation of the Strategy	**OCTOBER 1 STATUS** (If not implemented according to projected time frame, provide explanation.)
Action Step #3: Teachers will record the number of items and the location of the item on the inventory sheet.	☐G.4 ☒G.5 ☐G.6 ☐G.7	September 11, 2005 – September 30, 2005	Science Teachers as indicated above.	none	none	Completed inventories will be filed with Principal	
STRATEGY 7: Teachers will frequently include instructional methods and strategies by McREL and Marzano.	☐G.4 ☒G.5 ☐G.6 ☐G.7	September 2, 2005 – June 11, 2006	Science Teachers	none	Copies of "Instructional Methods Having A Strong Influence On student Achievement" and a listing of "Marzanno's Strategies"	Science Teacher's Lesson Plans	
Action Step #1: Teachers will refresh their understanding of McREL and Marzano.	☐G.4 ☒G.5 ☐G.6 ☐G.7	September 2, 2005	Science Teachers	none	Copies of the above lists	Lesson Plans	

Strategies and/or Action Steps	8 VAC 20-131-310 Code (place **x** by all that apply)	Projected Time Frame	**Person (s)** Responsible	**Financial Resources Needed (estimate amount and cite sources) G.9**	Other Resources Needed	Evidence of Implementation of the Strategy	**OCTOBER 1 STATUS** (If not implemented according to projected time frame, provide explanation.)
Action Step #2: Teachers will make a conscious effort to use these strategies as often as possible.	☐G.4 ☒G.5 ☐G.6 ☐G.7	September 2, 2005 – June 11, 2006	Science Teachers	none	Copies of the above lists	Lesson Plans	
Action Step #3: Teachers will stay focused on the data on the Disaggregator as they prepare lesson plans.	☐G.4 ☒G.5 ☐G.6 ☐G.7	September 11, 2005 – June 11, 2006.	Science Teachers as indicated above.	none	none	Completed inventories will be filed with Principal	
STRATEGY #8: Teachers will plan a Get Acquainted Program in the evening to make initial contact with parents.	☐G.4 ☒G.5 ☐G.6 ☒G.7	September 17, 2005 – and prior to November 5, 2005	Science Teachers Department Chairperson Librarian Scientists from "PASS"	none	School Calendar Science Teachers' Daily Lesson Plans	none	
Action Step #1: Check with administrator and clear a date for the meeting.	☐G.4 ☒G.5 ☐G.6 ☒G.7	September 17, 2005 – and prior to November 3, 2005	Department Chairperson	none	School Calendar Science Teachers' Daily Lesson Plans	none	

60

Strategies and/or Action Steps	8 VAC 20-131-310 Code (place **x** by all that apply)	Projected Time Frame	**Person (s)** Responsible	**Financial Resources Needed (estimate amount and cite sources) G.9**	Other Resources Needed	Evidence of Implementation of the Strategy	**OCTOBER 1 STATUS** (If not implemented according to projected time frame, provide explanation.)
Action Step #2: Teachers decide what will be presented.	☐G.4 ☒G.5 ☐G.6 ☒G.7	September 17, 2005 – and prior to November 3, 2005	Science Teachers Department Chairperson	none	School Calendar Science Teachers' Daily Lesson Plans	none	
Action Step #3: Teachers select a person to prepare flyers to send to parents	☐G.4 ☒G.5 ☐G.6 ☒G.7	September 17, 2005 – and prior to November 3, 2005	Science Teachers Department Chairperson	none	School Calendar Science Teachers' Daily Lesson Plans	none	
Action Step #4: Teachers complete logistics for the "Parent Night.	☐G.4 ☒G.5 ☐G.6 ☒G.7	September 17, 2005 – and prior to November 3, 2005	Science Teachers Department Chairperson Librarian Scientists from "PASS"	none	School Calendar Science Teachers' Daily Lesson Plans	none	

Strategies and/or Action Steps	8 VAC 20-131-310 Code (place **x** by all that apply)	Projected Time Frame	**Person (s)** Responsible	**Financial Resources Needed (estimate amount and cite sources) G.9**	Other Resources Needed	Evidence of Implementation of the Strategy	**OCTOBER 1 STATUS** (If not implemented according to projected time frame, provide explanation.)
STRATEGY 9: Teachers invite scientists for a day in each Science Classroom from PASS "Partnerships For Achieving Successful Schools"	☐G.4 ☒G.5 ☐G.6 ☒G.7	September 17, 2005 – and prior to November 3, 2005	Science Teachers Department Chairperson Librarian Scientists from "PASS"	none	School Calendar Science Teachers' Daily Lesson Plans	none	
Action Step #1: Teachers meet to decide which day during the first nine weeks that they prefer to invite "PASS".	☐G.4 ☒G.5 ☐G.6 ☒G.7	September 17, 2005 – and prior to November 3, 2005	Science Teachers Department Chairperson Librarian Scientists from "PASS"	none	School Calendar Science Teachers' Daily Lesson Plans	none	
Action Step #2: Department chairman checks the date with librarian who is the contact person for "PASS" and with the administrator.	☐G.4 ☒G.5 ☐G.6 ☒G.7	September 17, 2005 – and prior to November 3, 2005	Department Chairperson Librarian Administrator	none	School Calendar Science Teachers' Daily Lesson Plans	none	

Strategies and/or Action Steps	8 VAC 20-131-310 Code (place **x** by all that apply)	Projected Time Frame	**Person (s)** Responsible	**Financial Resources Needed (estimate amount and cite sources) G.9**	Other Resources Needed	Evidence of Implementation of the Strategy	**OCTOBER 1 STATUS** (If not implemented according to projected time frame, provide explanation.)
Action Step #3: All teachers and their students will participate.	☐G.4 ☒G.5 ☐G.6 ☒G.7	September 17, 2005 – and prior to November 3, 2005	Science Teachers Department Chairperson Librarian Scientists from "PASS"	none	School Calendar Science Teachers' Daily Lesson Plans	none	
STRATEGY 10: Teachers will prepare to do at least two hands-on activities per week.	☐G.4 ☒G.5 ☐G.6 ☐G.7	September 2, 2005 – June 11, 2006	All Science Teachers	Petty Cash funds	Science Teachers' Daily Lesson Plans Inventories of Materials and Equipment	Teachers' Daily Lesson Plans	
Action Step #1: Teachers will decide which experiments can be done to clarify or extend other instruction.	☐G.4 ☒G.5 ☐G.6 ☐G.7	September 2, 2005 – June 11, 2006	All Science Teachers	Petty Cash funds	Science Teachers' Daily Lesson Plans Inventories of Materials and Equipment	Teachers' Daily Lesson Plans	

Strategies and/or Action Steps	8 VAC 20-131-310 Code (place **x** by all that apply)	Projected Time Frame	**Person (s)** Responsible	**Financial Resources Needed (estimate amount and cite sources) G.9**	Other Resources Needed	Evidence of Implementation of the Strategy	**OCTOBER 1 STATUS** (If not implemented according to projected time frame, provide explanation.)
Action Step #2: Teachers will check to see that all materials are available.	☐G.4 ☒G.5 ☐G.6 ☐G.7	September 2, 2005 – June 11, 2006	All Science Teachers	Petty Cash funds	Science Teachers' Daily Lesson Plans Inventories of Materials and Equipment	Teachers' Daily Lesson Plans	
Action Step #3: Teachers will write the experiments chosen in their Daily Lesson Plans.	☐G.4 ☒G.5 ☐G.6 ☐G.7	September 2, 2005 – June 11, 2006	All Science Teachers	Petty Cash funds	Science Teachers' Daily Lesson Plans Inventories of Materials and Equipment	Teachers' Daily Lesson Plans	
Action Step #4: Subject area teachers will collaborate to be sure that there is enough materials or decide which day each teacher will do the lab.	☐G.4 ☒G.5 ☐G.6 ☐G.7	September 2, 2005 – June 11, 2006	All Science Teachers	Petty Cash funds	Science Teachers' Daily Lesson Plans Inventories of Materials and Equipment	Teachers' Daily Lesson Plans	

Strategies and/or Action Steps	8 VAC 20-131-310 Code (place **x** by all that apply)	Projected Time Frame	**Person (s)** Responsible	**Financial Resources Needed (estimate amount and cite sources) G.9**	Other Resources Needed	Evidence of Implementation of the Strategy	**OCTOBER 1 STATUS** (If not implemented according to projected time frame, provide explanation.)
STRATEGY 11: Teachers in each science subject area will collaborate to study and discuss the revised Science Standards and revise the curriculum accordingly.	☐G.4 ☒G.5 ☒G.6 ☐G.7	September 5, 2005	All Science Teachers	none	Revised SOL Standards for Science Original SOL Standards Chesapeake/ Petersburg Curriculum	Teachers' Daily Lesson Plans Menu for Opening of School Activities	
Action Step #1: Teachers will set a date to meet to discuss.	☐G.4 ☒G.5 ☒G.6 ☐G.7	September 5, 2005	All Science Teachers	none	Revised SOL Standards Original SOL Standards Chesapeake/ Petersburg Curriculum	Menu for Opening of School Activities	
Action Step #2: Teachers will compare the old standards with the new ones and note what is either added or deleted.	☐G.4 ☒G.5 ☒G.6 ☐G.7	September 5, 2005	All Science Teachers	none	Revised SOL Standards Original SOL Standards Chesapeake/ Petersburg Curriculum	Menu for Opening of School Activities	

Strategies and/or Action Steps	8 VAC 20-131-310 Code (place **x** by all that apply)	Projected Time Frame	**Person (s)** Responsible	**Financial Resources Needed (estimate amount and cite sources) G.9**	Other Resources Needed	Evidence of Implementation of the Strategy	**OCTOBER 1 STATUS** (If not implemented according to projected time frame, provide explanation.)
Action Step #3: Teachers will study the curriculum and add or delete as indicated by the standards.	☐G.4 ☒G.5 ☒G.6 ☐G.7	September 5, 2005	All Science Teachers	none	Revised SOL Standards Original SOL Standards Chesapeake/ Petersburg Curriculum	Menu for Opening of School Activities	

ADD ROWS AS NEEDED TO ACCOMMODATE NUMBER OF STRATEGIES
AND/OR APPROPRIATE NUMBER OF ACTION STEPS

REFERENCES

Guskey, T. R. (2005). *Formative classroom assessment and Benjamin S. Bloom: Theory, research, and implications.* Paper presented at the annual meeting of the American Educational Research Association, Montréal, Québec, Canada.
Retrieved December 9, 2006, from http://www.eric.ed.gov/ERICDocs/data/ericdocs2/content storage 01/0000000b/80/31/bb/33.pdf

Holcomb, E. L. (2000). *Asking the right questions: Techniques for collaboration and school change,* California: Corwin Press

O'Shea, M. R. (2005). From standards to success, *Association for Supervision and Curriculum Development, 2005.*

Phillips, D. T. (2000). Martin Luther King, Jr.: inspiration & wisdom for challenging times, Boston: Warner Books

Popham, W. J. (2006). All about accountability / Those [fill-in-the-blank] tests! *Educational Leadership, 63*(8), 85–86.

Reeves, D. B. (2006). The learning leader/How to focus school improvement for better results, Alexandria, VA: Association for Supervision and Curriculum Development (ASCD).

Shannon, G. S., & Bylsma, P. (2004). *Characteristics of improved school districts: Themes from research.* Olympia, WA: Office of Superintendent of Public Instruction. Retrieved December 9, 2006, from http://www.eric.ed.gov/ERICDocs/data/eric

Using the "No Child Left Behind Act" to improve schools in your state: A tool kit for business leaders. Information resources for business leadership to increase student achievement under the "No Child Left Behind Act of 2001." (2002). Washington, DC: Business Roundtable. (ERIC Document Reproduction Service No. ED468499)

U. S. Department of Education. (2001). No Child Left Behind: Executive Summary. Washington, DC: Author

Wilson, L. (2005). What every teacher needs to know about assessment, Larchmont, New York: Eye On Education

Wray, E (2013) RISE Model feedback tool, Retrieve from internet October 14, 2021 from file:///C:/Users/Thomas/Documents/RISE_rubric-peer.pdf

Printed in the United States
by Baker & Taylor Publisher Services